NUMBERS

Author

by Kity H.Q Steven

THIS BOOK BELONGS TO

....

1

One

2
two

3

Three

4

Four

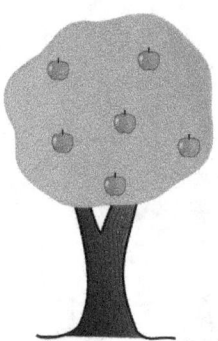 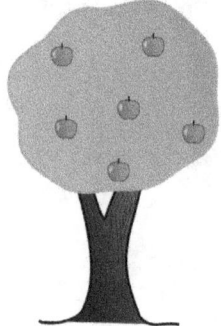

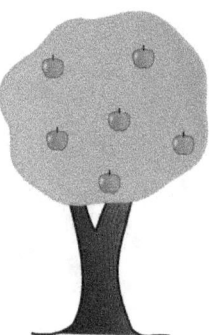 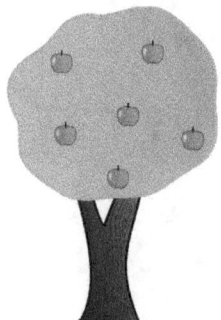

5

Five

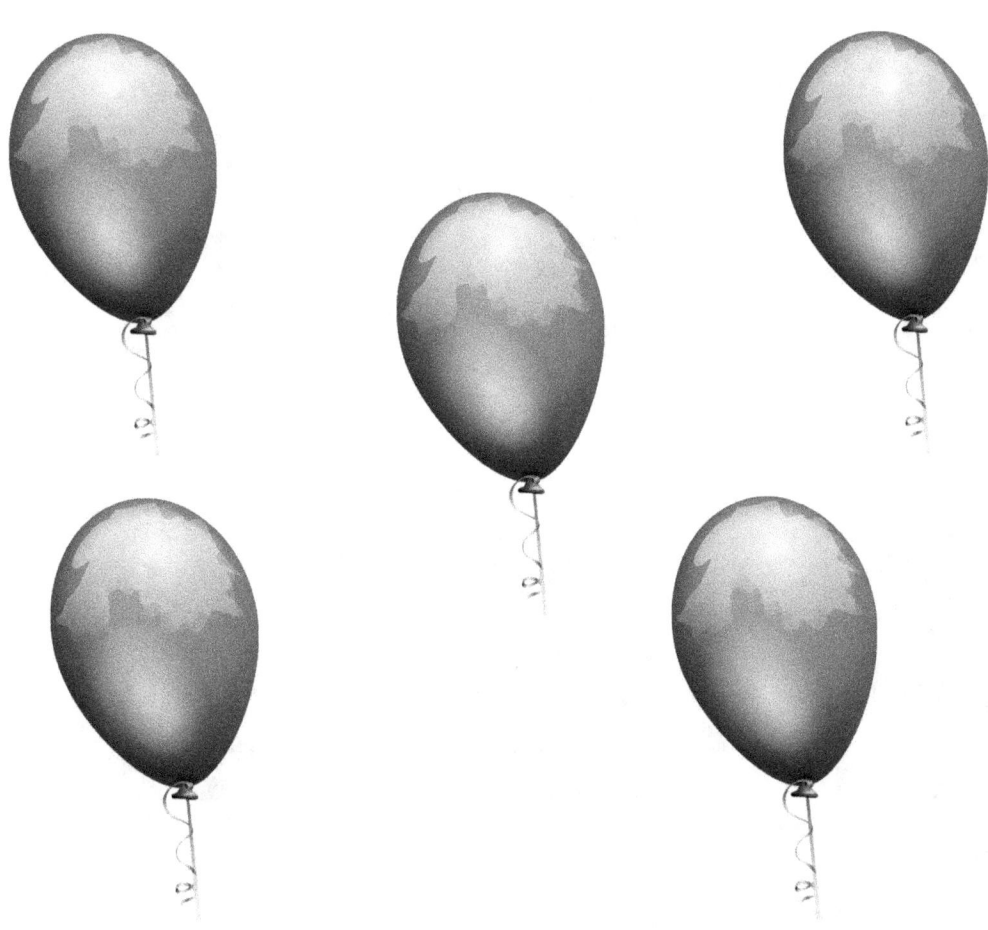

6

Six

7

Seven

8

Eight

10

Ten

One lamp

1 =

Two trains

2 =

Three tomatoes

3 =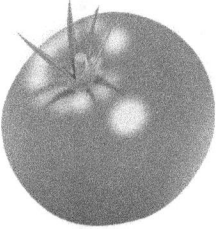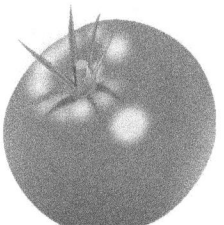

Four trees

4 =

Five bees

5 =

Six houses

6 =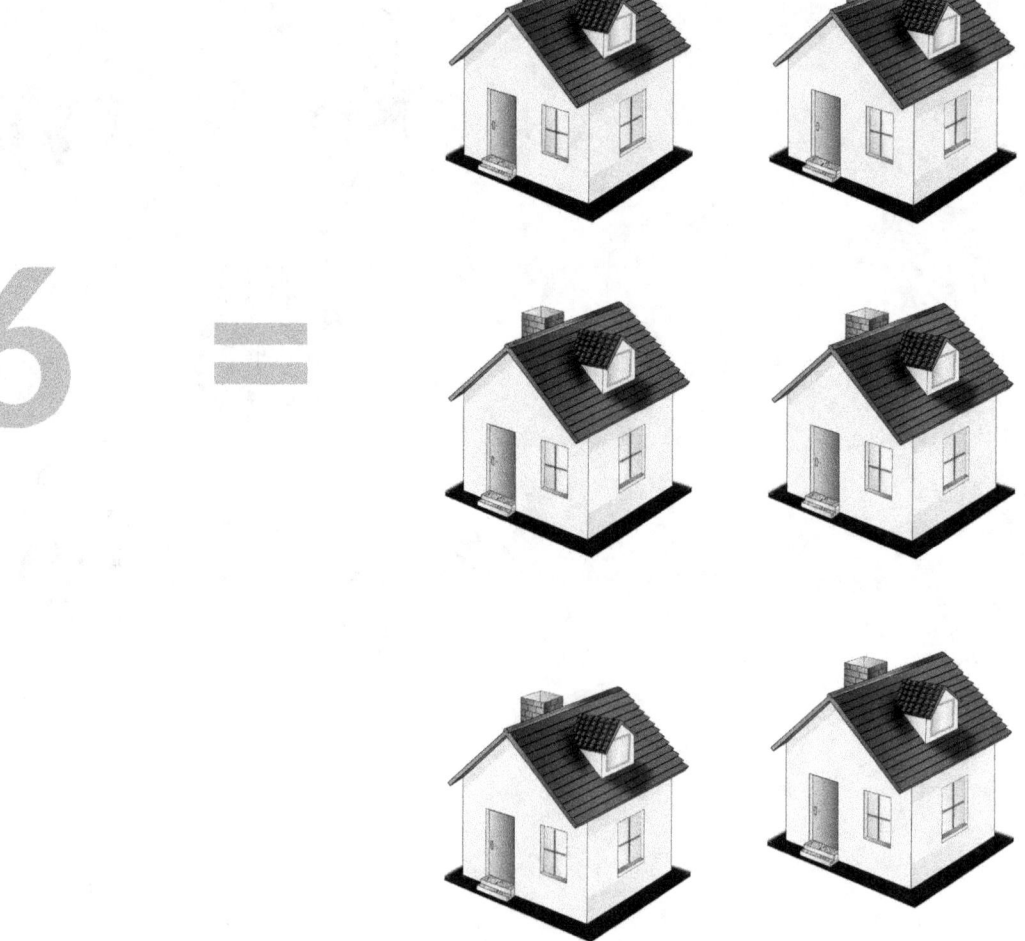

Seven cars

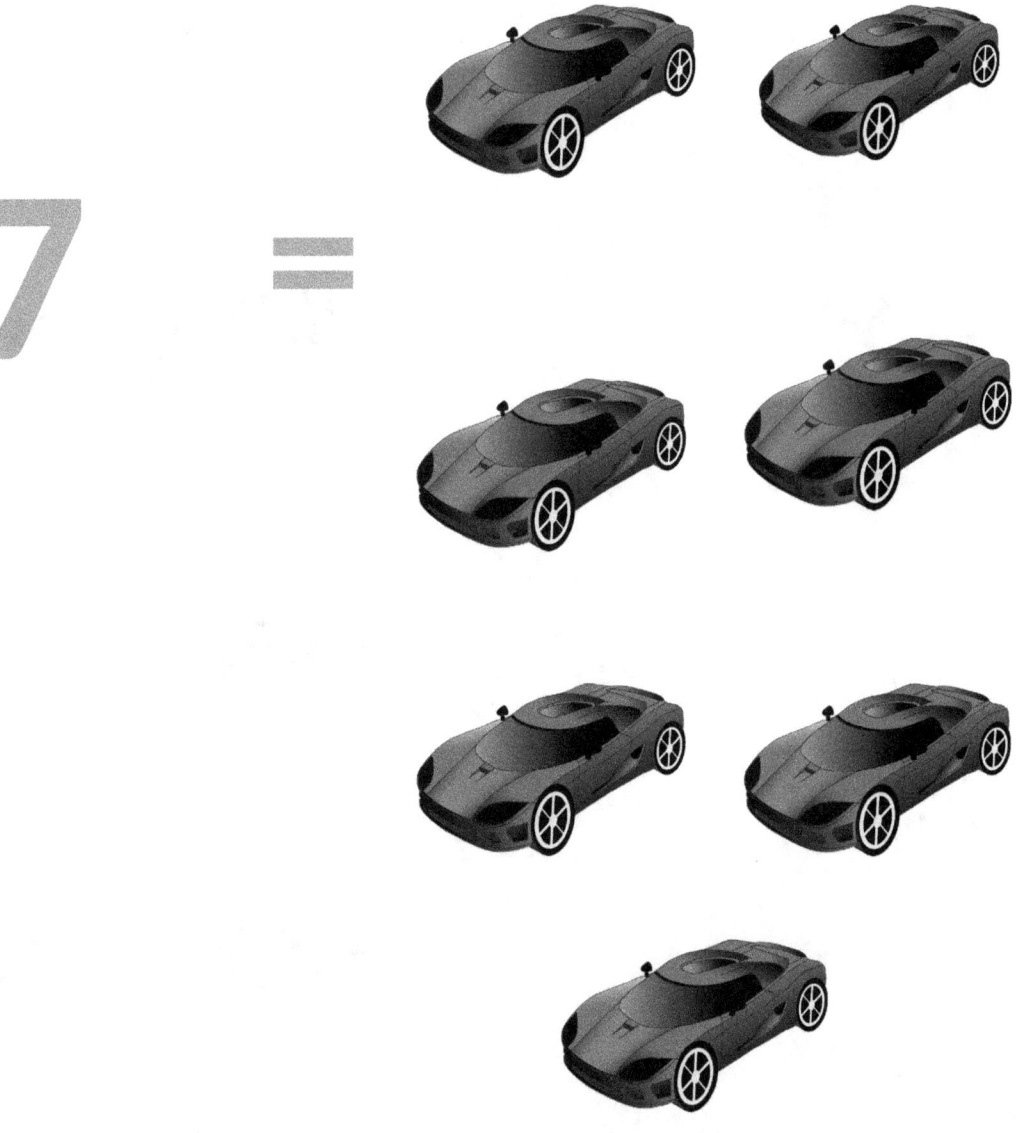

Eight umbrellas

8 =

Nine pencils

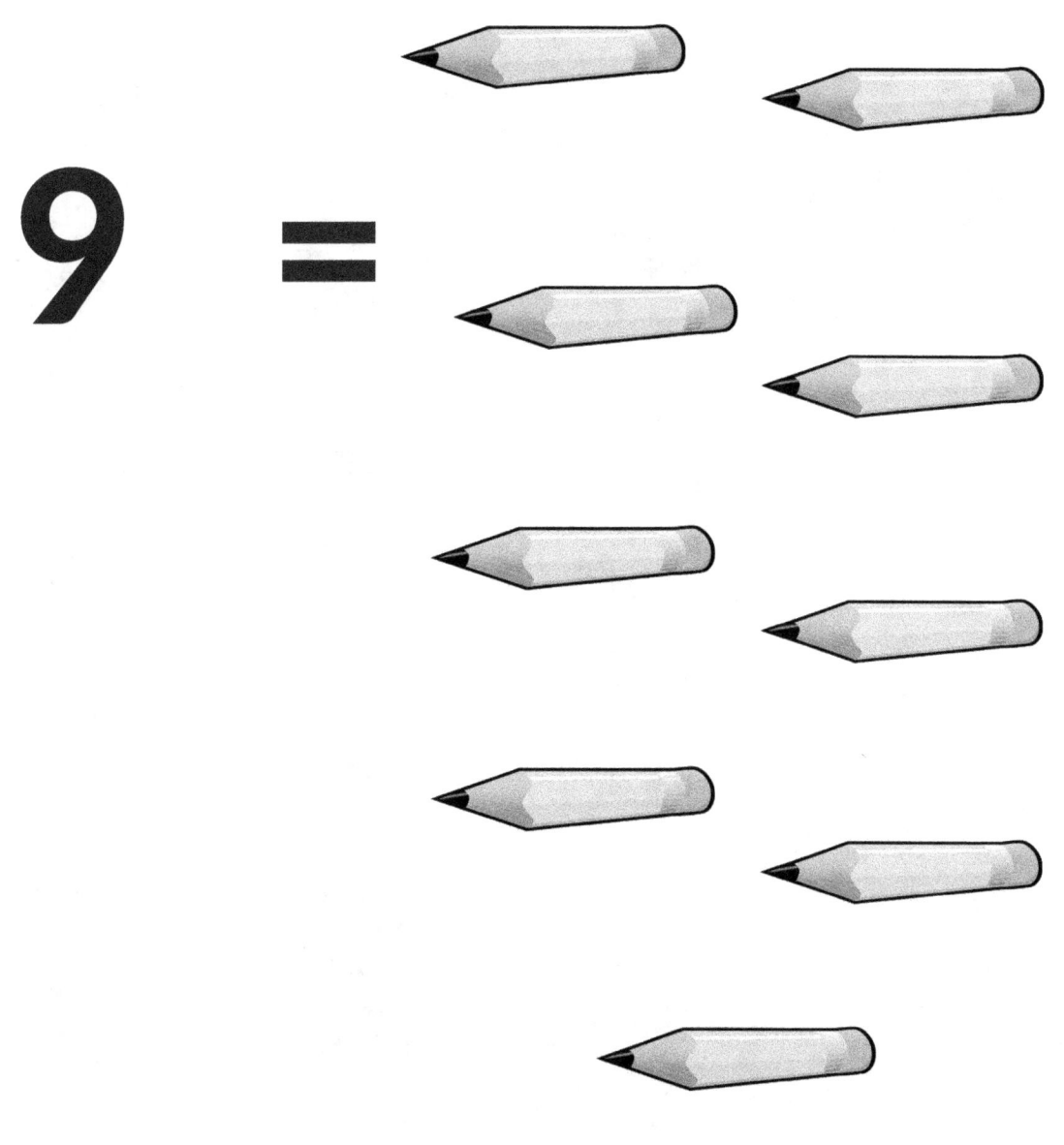

Ten giraffes

10 =

1 	**2** 
3 	4 

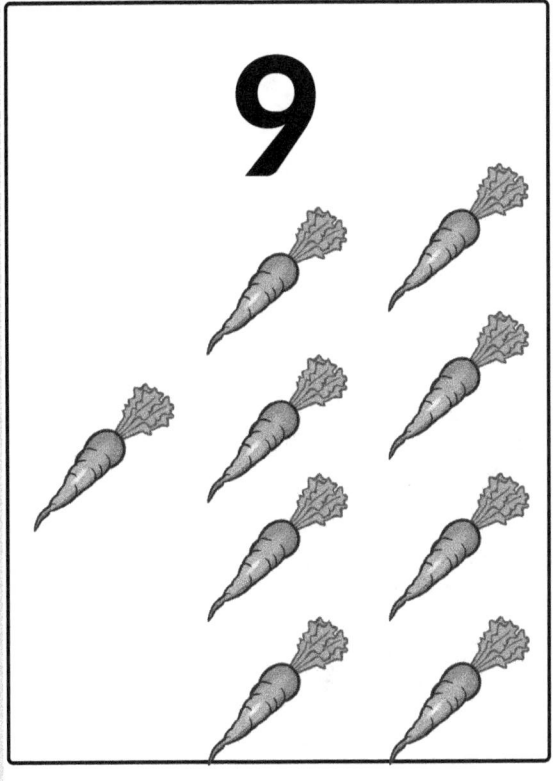

by Kity H.Q Steven

www.ingramcontent.com/pod-product-compliance
Lightning Source LLC
LaVergne TN
LVHW060134080526
838201LV00118B/3050